When Dreams Come True

The Story of Women Today Online

by *Katherine Kehler*
with *RuthAnn Raycroft*

"Over breakfast, Katherine expressed her continual desire to reach women and help them become all God wants them to be. A challenge was voiced to produce a book telling the many stories of women who have been touched through the Internet Ministry of Campus Crusade for Christ, Canada.

This book highlights just few of the thousands of people who have felt the hand of God on their life through the Internet ministry of Katherine Kehler and her team."

Henry and Laura Block
Langley, BC
Block Charitable Foundation
Board of Directors: Campus Crusade for Christ, Canada
Founding Member: Women Today, Canada

"Everyone needs a mentor, and Katherine Kehler has been a person in my life who has consistently modeled authentic Christianity. As a friend, co-worker, and a phenomenal leader, Katherine inspires many. In this book, Katherine will encourage and challenge you to be all God wants you to be."

Barbara Klemke
Edmonton, Alberta
The Klemke Foundation
Founding Member: Women Today, Canada

Edited by Idelette McVicker.
Cover design and illustration by Barton Pang.
Book design and graphics by Bob Canlas.

Scripture taken from the HOLY BIBLE, NEW INTERNATIONAL VERSION. Copyright 1973, 1978, 1984 International Bible Society. Used by permission of Zondervan Bible Publishers.

National Library of Canada Cataloguing in Publication Data

Kehler, Katherine
    When dreams come true : women today online
ISBN 1-55212-731-1
1. Self-actualization (Psychology) 2. Women—Psychology. I.
Raycroft. RuthAnn II. Title.

BF637.S4K43 2001   158.1'082   C2001-910643-2

TRAFFORD

This book was published *on-demand* in cooperation with Trafford Publishing. On-demand publishing is a unique process and service of making a book available for retail sale to the public taking advantage of on-demand manufacturing and Internet marketing. **On-demand publishing** includes promotions, retail sales, manufacturing, order fulfilment, accounting and collecting royalties on behalf of the author.

Suite 6E, 2333 Government St., Victoria, B.C. V8T 4P4, CANADA
Phone   250-383-6864   Toll-free   1-888-232-4444 (Canada & US)
Fax   250-383-6804   E-mail   sales@trafford.com
Website www.trafford.com
TRAFFORD PUBLISHING IS A DIVISION OF TRAFFORD HOLDINGS LTD.
Trafford Catalogue #01-0130   www.trafford.com/robots/01-0130.html

10   9   8   7   6   5   4   3   2

I dedicate this book
When Dreams Come True:
The Story of Women Today Online
to Marvin, my husband.

Throughout our 45 years of marriage
you have constantly encouraged me to use,
develop and multiply the talents God gave me.

So many times when I set out to
make one of my dreams become a reality,
it was you who motivated me
to keep focused on God's sufficiency—
and to keep going even when projects seemed overwhelming.

Marvin, thank you for believing in me.
Thank you for all of your support, motivation and encouragement.

Contents

Introduction

HAVE YOU EVER WONDERED WHY SOME WOMEN DREAM and leave no mark, while others dream and change the world?

Over the years I have spent a great deal of time talking to women. Many of them have shared with me the secret yearnings and unfulfilled longings they carry in their hearts. Their eyes sparkle as they tell me about an idea they may have been considering for years. Yet too often the tyranny of the urgent, lack of confidence or fear have held them back.

The passion these women share is inspiring: a woman with a desire to write children's books, a mother who wants to organize chapels for girls' synchronized swim teams, and a single woman who wants to reach fashion models for Christ. Yet I have been surprised and saddened to find that for so many, this passion rarely translates into action. Their dreams rarely make it to a list of five-year goals.

As I recognized the need to encourage women to pursue their dreams, I began to consider some of the women who had inspired me:

- Amelia Earhart dreamed of becoming the first woman to make both solo transatlantic and solo transcontinental flights in 1930.
- Dr. Henrietta C. Mears had dreams that influenced many of the great Christian leaders of our day including Dr. Billy Graham, Dr. William R. Bright and Dr. Richard Halverson.
- Pearl S. Buck was the first American woman to win the Nobel Prize for Literature in 1938.

There are so many wonderful examples of women who have turned their passions into accomplishments. It seems, though, that many women are waiting not only for a role model to point them in the right direction, but for someone to provide clear steps they can follow for determining what God wants to do with their dreams.

We all need a helping hand sometimes, to help us get started. Several years ago, as I prayed about this need, the Lord led me to devise and teach a seminar for women called "Accomplishing Your Dream." The seminar and the article that developed out of it, consisted of practical, prayerful and motivational techniques to help women turn dreams into reality.

In the pages to follow, I will share with you how God called me to a deeper relationship with Him. This intimate relationship gave me the confidence to:

- capture my dreams
- center on God

- face my foes
- count my assets
- go for the gold
- stay organized and on track.

I will share how these steps helped me turn my passion for reaching women into a successful Internet ministry impacting lives in over 160 countries around the world.

It is my prayer that the Lord will use these ideas and examples to inspire many more women to wholeheartedly pursue the passion He has placed in their hearts. If you have a dream, but are lacking the plan to make that dream come true, read on!

"Reach high,

for stars lie hidden in your soul.

Dream deep,

for every dream precedes the goal."

PAMELA VAULL STARR

"Do not conform any longer to the pattern of this

world, but be transformed by the renewing of your

mind. Then you will be able to test and approve what

God's will is—his good, pleasing and perfect will."

[Romans 12:2]

My Dreams Were Too Small

HERE CAN BE NO DISCUSSION OF KNOWING AND DOING God's will without some understanding of the relationship that makes such knowledge and action possible. The Lord will never give us a task, a dream or a passion we cannot see to completion through Him who gives us strength. Simply put, as believers in Christ we cannot begin to truly serve Him without surrendering to His Lordship over our lives.

I was a grown woman, the mother of four and a long-time Christian when the Lord revealed this simple truth to me. I believed in Christ, but I was in control of my own life. And I wasn't feeling fulfilled.

Many years ago, while dusting my bedroom dresser, I noticed a brochure. I picked it up and began reading, trying to decide whether to throw it away or file it. One phrase caught my attention: "Learn how to live the abundant Christian life."

The brochure was advertising a conference by an organization I had never heard of before: Campus Crusade for Christ. Initially I thought it was for college students. Certainly, I was too mature for such a conference, I thought.

Yet that phrase, "Learn how to live the abundant Christian life" kept coming to mind during the day. I had been a Christian since I was 12. Outwardly, I had everything a woman could possibly want:

- a wonderful, kind, handsome, generous husband
- four healthy children who did reasonably well in school
- our dream home (We had both been raised with a strong work ethic. We worked hard, God blessed us and we had gained some measure of success).

In the years prior to finding that pamphlet I had begun to sense that I was missing something. It started when my mother passed away. I missed her very much and I knew I wanted to see her again, but wasn't sure I would go to heaven when I died.

A few days after I read the brochure, my brother-in-law dropped in and asked if Marvin had mentioned the conference to me. I said "No," but that I was very interested. When my brother-in-law encouraged us to go, I listened. He had changed a lot in the previous few months. Even though he had always had a pleasing personality, he now radiated the joy of Christ. I really wanted that joy too.

When he left, I prayed, "God, how can I have this kind of joy?" The thought, "total commitment" crossed my mind, but I quickly pushed it aside. After all, I was already involved in many leadership roles in my church and community. I certainly didn't want more to do. But a quiet voice inside of me said, "I want you, not your work." I chose to ignore His voice then, but I didn't forget it. A few weeks later, Marvin and I were on our way to the conference.

During one of the messages, the speaker had us write a list of our acts and attitudes we knew were displeasing to God. I have to admit my list was much longer than I thought it would be. I then claimed the promise in 1 John 1:9, "If we confess our sins, He is faithful and just to forgive our sins and purify us from all unrighteousness." I felt so clean inside when I was done.

The next morning we heard the message on how to live a life filled with, or directed by, the Spirit. This was the moment of decision. In order to experience the abundant life I really wanted—in order to be filled with the Holy Spirit—I needed to give the control of my life to God. This time, I didn't hesitate.

I prayed a prayer that sounded something like this:

> Dear God, I need you. I know that I have sinned against you by directing my own life. I thank you that You have forgiven my sins through Christ's death on the cross for me. I invite Christ to again take His place on the throne of my life. Fill me with your Holy Spirit as you commanded me to be filled, and as You promised in Your word that you would do if I asked in faith. I pray this in the name of Jesus. As an expression of my

faith, I now thank You for directing my
life and for filling me with the Holy
Spirit. Amen.

Immediately, I was filled with such joy and love I couldn't contain myself. For a reserved person like me this was definitely supernatural.[1]

I realized I also had to decide that the Bible would be my authority from that day on. I would disregard anything that was not in agreement with God's Word.

That weekend Marvin and I committed our lives to help fulfill our Lord's Great Commission. Our priorities began to change. Our lives began to change. As hard as we had worked in our businesses, we now worked to reach our neighborhood, our country and the world with the good news of God's love and forgiveness.

Yet someone wisely said, "If your religion doesn't work at home, don't export it."

God changed my attitude. Once our son turned thirteen, we seemed to have a major crisis to deal with every three months and Marvin was away for many of them. I remember one occasion when I was very upset with my son because of something he had done. My attitude was wrong and I said unkind things to him. That night the Lord convicted me of my words and let me know I had to apologize. The next morning I did. My son graciously responded, "That's OK, Mom. None of us are perfect." I now know that listening to God and obeying when He speaks, is the key to having a relationship with Christ.

God is my strength. With Marvin travelling a lot during those years, I often felt lonely. One incident in particular stands out in my mind. He had been gone for two weeks and came home for the weekend because we were hosting a conference. We were both tied up with responsibilities all weekend. After the conference, I drove him to the airport—the car full of people. We hadn't had any time to ourselves. After I dropped him off and was driving home, I was ready for a major pity party. I prayed, "Lord, you have to help me."

That night, as I read my Bible, the words in Isaiah 40 comforted me. The Lord said to me through His word:

"You are my servant; I have chosen you and have not rejected you. So do not fear, for I am with you; do not be dismayed, for I am your God. I will strengthen you and help you; I will uphold you with my righteous right hand."

It was as though God put His arms around me and loved me. During those years He became dearer and nearer to me, and He continues to show me that He is in control. I know He will provide if I will listen, trust and obey.

When I was a young girl, my dream was to be married, have children and a lovely yard. My dreams were too small. Besides giving me those precious gifts, God wanted me to help change the world.

---

¹ If you would like to read more about how the Holy Spirit can give you power for living, go to Appendix I at the back of this book or visit "Have you made the wonderful discovery of the Spirit-filled life?" online at www.christianwomentoday.com/spiritfilledlife.html

"God hides some ideal in every human soul. At some

time in our life we feel a trembling, fearful longing to

do some good thing. Life finds its noblest spring of

excellence in this hidden impulse to do our best."

ROBERT COLLYER

"There is no magic in small plans. When I consider

my ministry, I think of the world. Anything less

than that would not be worthy of Christ

nor of his will for my life."

DR. HENRIETTA C. MEARS

CHAPTER TWO

Capture Your Dreams

AVE YOU EVER LOOKED AT YOUR LIFE AND WONDERED, "How did I get here?"

I'm not talking about the deliberate, sometimes unpleasant, self-inventory that many of us have had to make, particularly when life changes were in order. Instead, think of a moment of pure joy when an accomplishment or milestone that had seemed out of your reach was fulfilled. Were you a little surprised? I know I was.

In the year 2000, we at *Women Today Magazine* (www.womentodaymagazine.com) received some delightful news. *Webbound: The Essential Web Resource*, the #1 selling Internet Directory, had listed our website as one of the "Top 10 Women's Magazines" online. We were in good company, listed alongside the online versions of *Redbook* and *Good Housekeeping*. The listing was not unexpected because of the quality of the website (in fact, as Executive Editor, I am probably prone to bias).

No, the listing came as a wonderful surprise to me and my entire creative team, because of our magazine's purpose. *Women Today Magazine* is the evangelistic Website of the Women Today Internet ministry. In a market where nothing is sacred and everything is for sale, a website designed to point women to Christ had caught the attention of industry insiders.

Looking back at the journey we had taken to reach this point, I was filled with wonder. Had I envisioned this result when the ministry began? No, indeed. I could not have imagined what God was going to do through the Women Today Websites, or through me. When the Lord first directed my attention to the Internet, I was not interested in technology. The Information Super Highway was something I heard about from my co-workers, but I was not looking for a new project.

I did, however, have a passion.

My husband, Marvin, and I had prayerfully accepted leadership of Campus Crusade for Christ, Canada in 1974. Since that time, I had been led to found and give direction to several different movements within the Crusade family, including the Canadian Prayer Alert (providing resources on prayer, mobilizing intercessors and organizing a national prayer chain) and Women in Leadership (providing ministry to women in business and professional leadership roles). A busy mother and grandmother, I also travelled with my husband and worked toward the greater vision of the ministry as a whole.

Practically speaking, I probably had enough to do. Yet of all of these responsibilities, one idea kept me coming back. It was the nagging question that haunted my dreams: how could we reach more women for Christ and equip them to reach others?

God provided the framework I was looking for

through Women Today, a ministry of Campus Crusade for Christ, International started by Campus Crusade co-founder Vonette Bright. Women Today offered resources, tools and training more specific to women's lives. I brought the Women Today philosophy to Canada and, with like-minded women, set about to apply these approaches in our communities.

As this seed idea blossomed into a strategy, I invited women of influence to a meeting where I shared my dream to reach women for Christ. Many caught the vision and committed themselves to personal and financial involvement. At another rally and conference, Vonette came to challenge and inspire Christian women to reach their world for Christ. Many of these women responded as well. We followed up with growth and training seminars.

Women Today, Canada now offers accomplished and gifted women to speak to groups, large or small, about some aspect of their own lives or careers. In sharing a part of themselves, these speakers touch upon the needs common to women everywhere: career satisfaction, a happy family life, health, financial security, significance and self esteem, to name a few. With a bridge of understanding it is natural for the speaker to introduce Christ to the audience, share the changes that knowing Him has made and offer each of them the opportunity to know Him too.

In addition, we have implemented outreach strategies such as "Coffee Parties that Count," "Victorian Teas" and "International Women's Day," to encourage women to use hospitality as a tool for evangelism. Seminars are offered to help women walk daily in the power of the Holy Spirit, grow in their faith and learn how they could have a part in fulfilling the Great

Commission. Our staff offers their experience and wisdom in everything from writing an effective testimony to using tools such as tracts or videos.

Considering these tools, though, I saw another need to be filled. We needed a tool that women would be attracted to—something relevant to them. As I looked at various options, the Lord directed me to the supermarket checkout. What better way to reach women than a magazine!

Very soon, the first edition of *Women Today* was printed. Designed with the unchurched woman in mind, the magazine looked like something that women would pick up off a table in a waiting room, or select at that supermarket checkout. The articles covered a wide variety of issues that affect women's lives, written from a Christian perspective. We wanted a sensitive tool that women could confidently hand to their neighbors, knowing that the various articles would eventually lead the reader to the testimonies of Christian women and a clear gospel presentation. *(To order, turn to page 94.)*

God honored our faithfulness through these endeavors, and many women's lives were changed. Still, I could not help feeling that there was "more." The Lord had already done so many things that I could not imagine what else He had in store. Experience of His abundance, though, taught me to look forward.

In order to accomplish my dream, I needed to clarify my passion in my own mind.

· What did I want to have accomplished by the time I was 70 years old?
· Who would do it, if I didn't?
· Was there a target group or urgent need with

which God had burdened me?
- Were there some things that if I didn't do them, nobody would?
- Would the world be different because I pursued my passion?

To answer the first question, I looked back to the decision my husband and I had made to become part of Campus Crusade for Christ. As I matured in Christ and walked daily in the power of the Holy Spirit, my heart was burdened for the millions who had yet to turn to Him. I knew that I wanted to reach the lost and that I would be satisfied only with a life that had been spent serving Christ.

I knew, too, that the Lord had a very specific purpose for my life. The position with which He'd entrusted me involved certain responsibilities. He cautioned His disciples, and all of us who follow, that "the harvest is plentiful but the workers few."[1] As I asked myself "What will not get done if I do not do it?" I was reminded of a well-known illustration.

In *Things as They Are: Mission Work in Southern India*, published in 1903, missionary Amy Carmichael recounts a vision from a sleepless night. She perceived lost souls marching blindly toward a cliff, and a bottomless chasm. She watched helplessly as millions fell to their doom before she noticed that there were sentries along the edge of the cliff. Yet the sentries were spaced too far apart; they could not catch all of those who were going to fall or warn them of the danger. She noticed, too, that one of the sentries was called away and no one came to take her place. The gaps along the cliff were miles wide in some places, and though more sentries were called very few were willing. It is an excellent reminder that God wants to use each one of us to "stand in the gap" for those on their way to an eternity of darkness.

As for my particular burden, I could not deny that God had called me to minister to women. Nothing was accomplished through Women Today, Canada that He did not do. I was, and am, convinced that by sharing the gospel with women these efforts will be multiplied. My own family had taught me a great deal about the influence a woman has at home. My work with business and professional women gave me a clear indication of the impact that women can have at work and in the community.

My passion, then, was clear. Still, I was uncertain as to how God intended to develop it. The Lord required my patience and faith. I needed to focus my attention on Him and wait for Him to reveal His per-fect design in His time.

[1] Matthew 9:37, 38

ACTION POINTS

1. Make a list of the activities that capture your imagination or draw you back time after time. Gifting, character and individual spiritual journeys will lead us to be interested in many different things. There may be several ideas that offer you challenge and satisfaction. Is it the time you spend organizing activities for your son's volleyball team or is it the book manuscript you've had tucked away in your desk for over a year?

2. Ask yourself the questions from this chapter:
   —What do you want to have accomplished by the time you are 70 years old?

_____

_____

_____

_____

_____

   — Who would do it, if you didn't? Would the dream be left undone?

_____

_____

_____

_____

   — Is there a target group or urgent need with which God has burdened you?

_____

_____

_____

_____

   — Will the world be different because you pursued your passion?

_____

_____

_____

_____

_____

Add your answers to the list you've made.

3. Keep your list and your answers to these questions anywhere you will see them often. Pray continually that God will make it clear to you how He would like you to invest your passions. Pray for the leading of the Holy Spirit as you budget your time for all the activities you enjoy.

"God knows the secret plan

Of the things he will do for the world,

Using my hand."

TOYOHIKO KAGAWA

"Jabez cried out to the God of Israel,

'Oh that you would bless me and enlarge my territory!'

. . . And God granted his request."

[1 CHRONICLES 4:10]

CHAPTER THREE

Center on God

OD HONORED THE PRAYERS OF JABEZ, A MAN WHO WAS "more honorable than his brothers" (1 Chronicles 4:9). The Lord heard his earnest aspirations, and granted his request. What Jabez desired was within the bounds of God's will for his life and God's will for the people of Israel. It is remarkable how the Lord blesses us abundantly when our desires reflect His heart.

Dr. Henrietta C. Mears was a woman renowned for her intimacy with her Savior. From a young age, her greatest ambition was to know and do the will of God.

Ignoring her doctors, who predicted that she would be blind by the age of 30, Dr. Mears attended college and immersed herself in study. With an even greater zeal, she saturated herself with the word of God and prayed earnestly to be used. As she finished college and worked for several years, she continued to feel a calling to missionary work. It was a good plan and a worthy ambition, but it was not what the Lord had in mind.

She found herself in ministry at First Presbyterian Church of Hollywood. As the head of Christian education, Dr. Mears was dismayed to discover that the Sunday school material that had been ordered did not accurately teach what was found in Scripture. Her own desire to lead a life founded on Scripture made it impossible for her to accept Sunday school lessons that were anything less. With few other resources to choose from, she was forced to create her own brand new, firmly scriptural Sunday school curriculum. These lessons would later be published and distributed to other Christian educators, and influence generations of young people.

Dr. Mears had a dream to reach the lost. Though she was not called to the mission field herself, her unrelenting dedication to pursuing God's will for her life had a lasting impact on the world. Hundreds of the young people she mentored went on to full-time ministry.

As I sought the Lord's guidance for the passion He'd given me to reach women, He was faithful to answer my prayers. He had offered me a glimpse of His heart and began to show me the extent of His vision. Soon, my vision was expanded beyond the borders of my community and even my country. I was starting to see just how much "more" there really was, but I still needed a place to start.

I found it during a dessert evening for our organization's donors. George Pytlik, a local graphic designer and technology buff, gave a presentation that night on the potential for ministry on the Internet. I was struck by the facts he shared. Millions of souls, searching for information, entertainment and much more, were tapping into this new technology.

At that time, Internet researchers estimated that women made up approximately 35 percent of the online community, yet that number was expected to increase dramatically. It was predicted that by the year 2005, far greater than half of all Internet users would be women. Mainstream women's magazines were hurrying to finish the online versions of their publications in expectation of these changes. The potential audience was huge.

The dream God placed in my heart became a project I could not have envisioned. With the tools He provided, Women Today was poised to enter this new electronic mission field.

In 1995, with the help of Wendy and Karen Bowater, we launched the first Women Today Website as part of the Website of Campus Crusade for Christ, Canada. Similar to the print magazine, we offered an array of articles on various subjects. Testimonies from many women pointed to Jesus as Lord and Savior. There were shorter "potpourri" articles with tidbits of interesting information and helpful hints. There was even an advice column where readers could "Ask Andrea" questions.

Women Today Online grew, but there was so much more we could do to maximize the effectiveness of our efforts. One website offering a small selection of articles and testimonies, and maintaining a Christian overtone, could not possibly accomplish what I believed the Lord had in mind for this ministry. Non-

Christian women were unlikely to visit, and the needs of Christian women were only being met in part. It was clear that changes were necessary.

I knew that any changes we made had to be based on a clear mandate from the Lord. After much prayer, and searching Scripture, I soon felt confident that this was the direction the Lord was leading:

> "To the Jews I became like a Jew, to win the Jews. To those under the law I became like one under the law (though I myself am not under the law), so as to win those under the law. To those not having the law I became like one not having the law (though I am not free from God's law but am under Christ's law), so as to win those not having the law. To the weak I became weak, to win the weak. I have become all things to all men so that by all possible means I might save some. I do all this for the sake of the gospel, that I may share in its blessings."
>
> 1 Corinthians 9:20-23

> "But since we belong to the day, let us be self-controlled, putting on faith and love as a breastplate, and the hope of salvation as a helmet. For God did not appoint us to suffer wrath, but to receive salvation through our Lord Jesus Christ . . . Therefore encourage one another and build each other up, just as in fact you are doing."
>
> 1 Thessalonians 5:8, 9, 11

Christ's commandment to make disciples has always been at the heart of our mission statement: to win women to Christ, build them in their faith, train them and send them to win, build, train and send others. Soon, one website became two. The original website was redesigned and renamed *Christian Women Today* (www.christianwomentoday.com). With more resources available online, greater access to tools and training and more fellowship, this magazine aimed to meet believers where they are and encourage them to continue their journey of faith.

A new Website was specifically designed for evangelism — to capture the attention of the unchurched woman. *Women Today Magazine* (www.womentoday-magazine.com) continued the same "lifestyle" emphasis as the print magazine and Christian Women Today. The difference with the new site was that every effort was made to avoid terms and phrases commonly used among Christians, but have little meaning to the unchurched.

The content of the Women Today Websites, and particularly the evangelistic magazine, needed to find the common voice of women on the Internet. Concise articles, touching on topical concerns without compromising our Christian perspective and mission statement, became the priority. The articles and features were gleaned from a variety of sources including submissions, reprinted articles, commissioned stories and interviews. Articles were frequently interlinked, helping the reader to find information on the website related to similar topics. This is also a great way to draw readers toward an exploration of spiritual issues.

One edition of *Women Today Magazine* featured a brief, fact-based story on a common women's health issue. At the end of this article, the reader was invited to enjoy another related story. This story from a Canadian writer dealt with her own experience in seeking help for this health issue. Her trip to the doctor's office gave rise to a question of morality; the doctor assumed that as a single woman she would be sexually active and prone to other conditions. Her choices, and the faith that influenced them, took center stage. Her light-hearted approach to the many benefits of her choice became the perfect introduction to an in-depth article about the Christian perspective on sexuality. Readers were also directed to a related testimony, and to a gospel presentation.

We want to meet women where they are, and encourage them to begin or deepen their relationship with Christ. In order to accomplish these goals, it is vital that the Women Today Websites remain relevant. We want to do our part to ensure the effectiveness of the ministry— to offer readers the content and features that they want without sacrificing the truth—and leave the results to God.

Dr. Bill Bright, founder of Campus Crusade for Christ stated, "Whatever we vividly envision, ardently desire, sincerely believe, and enthusiastically act upon must inevitably come to pass, provided there is a scriptural authority for it." I knew that nothing I undertook could be successful without this confirmation. I wanted to see the Women Today Websites grow, but only in the direction the Lord had ordained.

By centering on God, and seeking His will for my dream, God made it possible to fully explore the potential of this ministry on the Internet. I was excited to see what He would bring to pass, but not everyone shared my enthusiasm.

ACTION POINTS

1. Consider the dream in your heart and ask yourself the following: is this dream from God or is it your own desire?

—What eternal significance does your dream have?

_____
_____
_____
_____
_____
_____
_____
_____

—How will it make a difference in light of eternity?

_____
_____
_____
_____
_____
_____
_____
_____

When we do the will of God—what He prepared you for and put you on earth for—you don't have to worry about anything. Your responsibility is to be all God made you to be and to do with all your strength what God has given you to do today. Don't let a desire for praise or status cloud your purpose.

2. Who or what motivates you to accomplish your dream?

_____

_____

_____

_____

_____

_____

3. Why is it important to you to see this dream ful-filled?

_____

_____

_____

_____

_____

_____

_____

_____

_____

_____

4. Identify the biblical basis for your dream. God will never give you a dream that conflicts with the teaching of Scripture.

_____

_____

_____

_____

_____
_____
_____
_____
_____
_____
_____
_____
_____
_____

5. Has God revealed any Scripture to you regarding this specific dream? Add this to your dream work-sheet.

_____
_____
_____
_____
_____
_____
_____
_____
_____
_____
_____
_____
_____
_____
_____
_____

"Success is not measured by what a man accomplishes,

but by the opposition he has encountered and the

courage with which he has maintained the struggle

against overwhelming odds."

CHARLES LINDBERGH

"Don't doubt in the darkness what God has given you

in the light."

DR. HENRIETTA C. MEARS

CHAPTER FOUR

Face Your Foes

MELIA EARHART'S NAME IS SYNONYMOUS WITH THE early daredevil days of aviation. Her life, her records as a pilot, and her disappearance while attempting to circumnavigate the globe are legendary. Yet thinking about the things she was able to accomplish, I couldn't help but wonder about the path she had followed to get there.

Born in 1897 in Atchison, Kansas, Amelia Earhart was the older of two daughters. Adventurous and active, she and her sister might have been considered unusual in an era when women generally were confined to quieter activities. As a young woman, Amelia attended a flying exhibition with her mother and was immediately entranced by air travel. But women pilots were not common. In fact, her first attempt to find a flying instructor failed.

Money was certainly an issue and flying lessons were expensive. Amelia was a college student. Her family was unable to help; years of marital problems had left her parents very poor. They were perhaps also unwilling to devote precious funds to such an impractical pastime.

Amelia was undaunted. Eventually she found a well-known female pilot willing to teach her and willing to accept payment on installment. With moderate help from her mother's inheritance money, Amelia saved to buy her first airplane.

It wasn't long, though, before she faced another challenge. In 1924, her parents' marriage finally collapsed. Amelia postponed her dream to fly and took a teaching job near her mother. In 1926, she began working as a social worker in Massachusetts. She was still working at Dennison House in Boston, teaching English to immigrant children, when the opportunity arose to resume her career as a pilot.

Social conventions, financial struggles and family problems might have changed what we know about the history of air travel. Amelia Earhart might never have become an aviation pioneer. Yet she overcame setbacks and pursued her dream with conviction and passion. She set many records, including a speed record for the first transatlantic flight piloted by a woman.

There is a wonderful freedom in knowing with certainty what you have been called to do. There can be an equal frustration when circumstances or discouragement prevent you from reaching your goals. Roadblocks, though, don't stop traffic forever. They are a temporary diversion. They can be removed.

As I proceeded to pursue my dream of reaching women on the Internet, I was faced with some of these "temporary diversions." The first roadblock was my own lack of experience with the technology. I had never really used the Internet and knew very little about how it worked. I could not gauge how the website would function, how much it would cost or what skills the staff would need to have. Experience would prove to be the best teacher.

I was reminded of something I had heard years before. At the seminar where my husband, Marvin, and I first learned about the Spirit-filled life, someone said, "God is not interested in your ability. He is only interested in your AVAILability." It wasn't up to me to decide what I was or was not capable of. God had called me to this work, and He would enable me to do it. Comforted and confident, I undertook to learn what I could and trusted the Lord to provide the expertise we would need.

The need for technical expertise was the second roadblock. Initially, I relied heavily on the Computer Services department at Campus Crusade for Christ, Canada for information and help. George Pytlik, whose presentation on the Internet had so inspired me, agreed to design the website. It was a great start, but it soon became clear, that the Women Today Website would require a complete, dedicated staff.

As the ministry grew it outpaced my ability to get

the help we needed. Without a permanent staff member to oversee the website, I did not see how we could accomplish this dream. Our greatest need was for a Webmaster, someone with the skills to run the site and the knowledge to see what we needed. I prayed for the Lord to provide someone to guide the design and maintenance of the Website, and He responded abundantly.

I received an email from a young man who worked near our headquarters. Brent Purves was excited about our mission and impressed by what we had accomplished so far. However, he believed he could do it better. I met with him to see if he could live up to his sales pitch. His creativity and excitement were contagious and his expertise was a perfect match for our needs. It was very clear that God had delivered our Webmaster.

The Women Today Websites now had a staff of three, but there was still so much we needed. A great deal of time and many gifts are involved in putting together a successful website. The content alone requires full-time attention, both to write new material and to find existing articles that meet the criteria to win, build, train and send. Many Christian writers had made their work available to us, as part of their tithe and as an outpouring of their gifts. These submissions must be read and edited. Again, the Lord blessed us abundantly by bringing several talented women, including RuthAnn Raycroft (who helped me with this book) to manage the content for Women Today Online, as well as Dr. Ginger Gabriel, a family counselor from California.

There were, and continue to be, needs in other areas. We needed someone to answer general inquiries, send follow-up material and keep track of the statistics for the Websites. Soon the Lord led someone to fill this position. As we explored the possibilities of opening a chat room, it became clear that we would need someone to moderate these discussions. The Lord provided two talented and dedicated women to oversee this new venture and encourage prayerful women to join them in mentoring those who are struggling. As we stepped out in faith, God continued to meet our needs.

The next roadblock I faced was less concrete. In addition to facing tangible deficiencies, I was faced with a general lack of knowledge about the Internet among Christian women. Not everyone was as convinced as I was that we were on the right track.

The Internet was, and likely still is, a highly suspect media within Christian circles. The truth is that the Internet has, much to Satan's delight, been used for many dark purposes. There is no denying that many lives have been damaged by what is available in cyberspace, however the same can be said of other media like magazines and television. The Internet was beginning to be used by many Christian organizations and individuals to share the good news of Jesus Christ. Even so, many people with whom I shared my dream were skeptical. They had a lot of questions.

Would anyone really read a magazine about Jesus on the Internet? Were there enough women on the Internet to make this necessary? Wouldn't it be safer to undertake evangelism using some method that had already proven effective? Was this an effective use of the money donors entrusted to us for spreading the gospel?

Even the design and content of the website came under fire: many Christians thought that the website was far too "secular," while others thought it was far too "churchy." Yet, as difficult as it was to find believers who shared my vision for the Internet, it was not impossible. As the Lord continued to overcome our roadblocks, He continued to strengthen me in the face of discouragement.

Without a Webmaster, an editor, or donors who believed in the possibilities of reaching and discipling women on the Internet, Women Today Online might have ended. But I was convinced that the Lord had ordained this ministry. I had focused my dream on Him, and He had led me forward. Claiming His promises, I was able to turn and face the discouragement that might have stopped me.

ACTION POINTS

1. List the "roadblocks" that are preventing you from accomplishing your dream:

    — A lack of encouragement?
    — A lack of training or skills?
    — Fear of failure?
    — Lack of funds or resources?
    — A schedule that is already full?
    — Anything else?

_____

_____

_____

_____

_____

2. Consider the list for a moment. Are these road-blocks the Lord can help you to overcome? Is there anything you have written down that might not be a roadblock at all, but is a deception of the enemy?

_____

_____

_____

_____

_____

_____

_____

_____

3. Pray diligently over this list. Trust that the Lord will be faithful to help you accomplish what He has called you to do and overcome any obstacles in your path. Keep track of the ways in which the Lord is removing the roadblocks.

_____

_____

_____

_____

_____

_____

_____

_____

_____

"What we are is God's gift to us.

What we become is our gift to God."

LOUIS NIZER

"And along with the dream, will You give me

whatever graces, patience, and stamina it takes

to see the dream through to fruition?"

CATHERINE MARSHALL

CHAPTER FIVE

Count Your Assets

F ACING YOUR FOES AND PRESSING FORWARD TAKES tremendous courage. Judging by the struggles that so many of us have with self-esteem this next step may prove even more challenging.

You will undoubtedly face roadblocks as you pursue the dream the Lord has for you, causing you to cling more tightly to Him every step of the way. God has prepared you for the work to which He calls you. You are uniquely suited to the task, and He will provide you with all the resources you may need. It is up to you—to each one of us— to recognize these gifts, and make the most of them.

Pearl S. Buck may be familiar to you as the author of "The Good Earth", which won a Pulitzer Prize in 1935 and was made into a movie of the same name in 1937. In fact, she

was the author of over 180 works of fiction
and became the first American woman to win
the Nobel Prize for Literature in 1938.

What you may not know is that Pearl S.
Buck was also a well-known philanthropist.
She helped to create cultural understanding
between China and the West and founded the
first international, interracial adoption
agency in the United States.

Pearl Comfort Sydenstricker Buck was
born in the United States while her missionary parents were home on furlough. One of
only three of the Sydenstricker children to
live to adulthood, she spent the first half of
her life in China and was bilingual from an
early age. Though she would later reject the
tenets of the religion with which she had been
raised, she would pursue the causes of social
justice, civil and women's rights with zeal.

The lifetime of first-hand experience that
informed her writing shaped her ideals as
well, from teaching battered women sewing
and knitting skills in a shelter in Shanghai to
travelling westward through the poverty-
stricken Russian countryside on her way to
college in the U.S. Her interest in the welfare
of children stemmed not only from these
experiences, but also from her own adoption
of seven children. Welcome House, the adoption agency she founded in 1949, and the
Pearl S. Buck Foundation, founded in 1964
to provide support for Amerasian children
not eligible for adoption, continue her work
to this day.

A child of two cultures, Pearl S. Buck strove to demystify the "East" and bridge the gap between China and America. In 1949, she and her husband founded the East and West Association, dedicated to cultural exchange. She also helped discussion about mental handicaps and mental illness by writing a book about her own mentally handicapped daughter.

Pearl S. Buck had experience and understanding that few women of her time could claim. She had resources that few others could access. Whatever modern critics may make of her body of work as a writer, there is no denying that Pearl Buck made the most of what she had been given and went on to have a significant impact on her world.

As I trusted the Lord to provide the things we needed and did not yet have, and as I witnessed His answers to prayer, I was prompted to consider the things He had already provided for my dream. I made an inventory of these blessings by answering the following questions.

What are my resources?

I quickly learned that the first and most apparent of the resources God had provided, is the Internet itself. This network of information and ideas already served to accelerate the spread of the gospel in some very interesting places: "closed" countries, multinational organizations, political institutions, universities and schools. The possibilities are endless.

The United Nations Headquarters, for instance,

covers 18 acres on the East Side of Manhattan in New York City. Comprised of four main buildings, designed by an international team of 11 architects, the complex is an international zone belonging to all member states. It has an international staff and security force; it has a fire department and its own postal administration (which issues UN stamps that can only be mailed from the headquarters). There are representatives from 188 member nations. It is a mission field unto itself.

In the Spring of 2000 we received a response from the French translation of *Women Today Magazine* (www.femmesaujourdhui.com). The woman who wrote had carefully filled in the questionnaire so that we could send her more information. Her note had been sent to Anne-Marie Montgomery, a French-speaking volunteer in Ontario, Canada who had taken on the follow-up for the French website. Though none of us in the office at the time could translate the message, one thing was clear—her mailing address: UN Plaza, New York.

"Michelle was the first person who requested more information," Anne-Marie wrote to us later. "She works for the UN in a country in Africa and she said she wanted to pray the prayer, but had questions on the existence of evil and suffering."

Anne-Marie emailed her a few thoughts on the subject. Their relationship began to grow and for several weeks they corresponded on this one issue.

"After a few weeks," Anne-Marie continued, "she indicated that she had finally understood that we were saved by grace."

Since then, Michelle has asked many more questions. She and her new mentor continue to correspond about once a week as she grows in her newfound faith.

"We have talked about forgiveness, divorce, giving thanks in all circumstances," Anne-Marie said. "We just basically share what we are living and learning in Christ. I am seeing in her a thirst for God and a desire to grow that is so encouraging. Her last letter about practicing giving thanks in all circumstances was so refreshing."

The Internet is a wonderful tool for reaching those who might not have been reached by other means. It is also a very useful tool for those who live in remote areas, who live with physical challenges, illness, or are housebound. The Internet is particularly valuable where religious freedom is limited or threatened.

In countries where Christianity is actively repressed, online presentations of the gospel are still available in universities, libraries, businesses, government agencies and many more homes than you might expect. Many governments—from Saudi Arabia to the United States—have expressed concern over the kinds of information made available to their citizens. Yet the fact remains that the vast resources of the Internet are difficult to censor or trace making it possible to openly share the gospel.

Early in 2000 we learned that two individuals in Iran had made use of this open door. We received two response cards from the printed *Women Today* magazine. A man and a woman, one a young professional and the other a graduate student, had each ordered the free magazine after visiting our evangelistic website. Each of them indicated that they had prayed to invite Christ into their lives and requested more information to help them grow.

The anonymity of the Internet has been used for many dark purpose—what the Bible refers to as "what the disobedient do in secret" (Ephesians 5:12). Yet it can also afford the hurting and the seeking a safe place to ask questions without being judged or exposed. Privacy is a primary consideration for the Internet community.

The particular nature of the need for privacy among those who use the Internet, and the widespread impact of this medium, became apparent during an evangelistic campaign in Vancouver, Canada. Television and radio commercials, billboards and other ads expressed the difference a personal relationship with Christ had made in the lives of many individuals. Viewers were offered two alternatives for more information: a toll-free telephone number and the address for a website.

At the end of the campaign, organizers received an email from a young couple. Kevin and Cathy shared that they had come to Christ and recently been baptized in a local church as a result of the campaign. Kevin explained that they had responded to the ads through the website, because it was "anonymous and non-threatening." He said that, "One's faith is a very personal, very delicate thing." Kevin and Cathy were not alone—three out of every four people who responded to the campaign did so by visiting the website.

How has God uniquely prepared me for my dream?

Having already come to the conclusion that God did not require my ability but only my AVAILability, I was no longer concerned about what I lacked. Instead, I took stock of all the gifts He had given me that I could now commit to His use in this new endeavor.

- I am a leader, and already had experience direct-ing other ministries.
- I have a burden for reaching women and God had already blessed me with experience in doing so.
- I am wholly committed to doing whatever God wants me to do, and have frequently stepped out in faith with little more than the conviction that He had called me.

I am also blessed with a husband who shares my passion for reaching the lost. Marvin is my biggest supporter and my greatest encouragement. Working with him has been a wonderful faith adventure. We have learned to expect God to do the unexpected, whether in ministry or in our lives.

In addition to this personal growth, our work pro-vided some very tangible assets for the dream God had given me.

- I had received training in evangelism.
- I had access to the experience and wisdom of the world-wide Crusade organization.
- I was familiar with many tools and resources that could be partnered with a new Internet venture.
- I had experience raising the funds necessary to sustain a new ministry.
- I have travelled to many countries which has helped me have a global vision.

There was no question in my mind that God had called me to fulfill this dream. He had provided for all of the apparent liabilities we faced. An inventory of the ways in which He had prepared for this new ministry confirmed His leading and His ability to accomplish the tasks ahead.

Besides the resources He had provided, and the gifts and abilities He had given me, I was reminded that the Lord Himself is the only resource we need. He has given each of us His Holy Spirit and His Word. As my team and I forged ahead, we could, with absolute confidence, repeat His promise found in I Thessalonians 5:24: "The one who called you is faithful and He will do it."

ACTION POINTS

1. Look at your notes at the end of Chapter Three. How many of these "liabilities" has God provided for? How has He already answered your prayers?

_____

_____

_____

_____

2. Ask yourself the questions from this chapter, and list at least one item for each:

—How has God uniquely prepared you for your dream?

_____

_____

_____

_____

— How is your personality suited to this dream?

_____

_____

_____

_____

_____

—What particular skills or knowledge have you gained that will help you accomplish your dream?

_____

_____

_____

_____

_____

—How will the people in your circle of influence impact or be impacted by your dream?

_____

_____

_____

_____

_____

—Is there an aspect of your heritage that may provide the contacts or insight you need to pursue your dream?

_____

_____

_____

—How have your life experiences prepared you for
your dream?

_____

_____

_____

_____

_____

—Have God's financial blessings put you in a position to pursue your dream?

_____

_____

_____

_____

—What special gifts has the Lord provided that you
will need for your dream?

_____

_____

_____

_____

—What are your resources?

_____

_____

_____

_____

_____

—Do you have a mentor?

_____

_____

_____

_____

_____

—What about the team of people you are working with? List all of the resources you can think of.

_____

_____

_____

_____

_____

2. Remember that the Lord promises to be faithful to accomplish whatever He has called you to do. Make a list of similar promises from Scripture, and commit them to memory. Here are some to get you started:

1 Thessalonians 5:24	John 15:5
Matthew 6:33-34	John 5:17, 19-20
Psalm 20:7	Philippians 2:13
Proverbs 19:21	Ephesians 4:15-16
Mark 10:27	Mark 11:24
John 14:10	Philippians 1:6

"There is no magic in small plans.

When I consider my ministry, I think of the world.

Anything less than that would not be worthy of Christ

nor of his will for my life."

DR. HENRIETTA C. MEARS

"Therefore, since we are surrounded by such a great

cloud of witnesses, let us throw off everything that

hinders and the sin that so easily entangles, and let us

run with perseverance the race marked out for us.

Let us fix our eyes on Jesus, the author and perfecter

of our faith, who for the joy set before him endured

the cross, scorning its shame, and sat down at the right

hand of the throne of God."

[HEBREWS 12:1-2]

CHAPTER SIX

Go for the Gold

O LYMPIC ATHLETES CAN SPEND A LIFETIME PREPARING for one opportunity to win a gold medal. They endure demanding physical training. They sacrifice their time as well as other activities they might enjoy. They dedicate themselves to a grueling routine.

Is it worth it? One look at the face of an athlete standing on the podium as their national anthem plays and the answer must be a resounding, "Yes!" In an instant, all the challenges of the journey they took to reach the Olympics become worthwhile.

Silken Lauman started training as a rower when she was 11 years old. For years her life was focused on one goal—to reach the Olympic games and win a medal for Canada.

On the road to accomplishing her dream, she hit a roadblock. During a practice run, Silken was hit by another water-goer and her leg was severely injured. It seemed unlikely that she would completely heal and return to competition.

After painful recuperation, healing the damage to her leg and returning her body to peak condition, Silken Lauman came back. We all watched with admiration as she pushed her body to its limits, never taking her eyes off of the prize before her. Just 10weeks after the accident, she took home a bronze medal. Her satisfaction with the outcome was profound, because she had not only won a medal but had achieved her personal goals.1

Silken Lauman is a champion, a woman of courage and perseverance. As spectators, we saw not only the triumph at the finish line, but the single-minded determination it took to get there. As we work to accomplish our own dreams, we can find inspiration in her success.

In Hebrews, our life on earth is compared to a race. Like an Olympic athlete we must persevere, allowing nothing to prevent us from doing that to which Christ has called us. And, like Silken Lauman, we must run this race passionately with our eyes fixed on the prize. As Christians, our "prize" is Christ Himself, and an eternity spent with Him in the presence of His Father.

Accomplishing your dream requires more than enthusiasm, although that is a good place to start. But how will you run the race? And how will you finish?

Once you have clarified your passion and determined that you are pursuing God's will for your life, you will have to overcome some roadblocks. Not everyone will understand what you are doing. Fortunately, each of us has assets that can help us accomplish our goals. Time spent cataloguing the things you already have going for you, and considering how they will help you, will encourage you to continue.

Now it is time to set some goals.

As Silken Lauman pursued her dream, the goals she set for herself along the way helped her to push forward. Goals help us to stay motivated and to measure the progress of our efforts. There are three types of goals that I recommend:

— One-month goals
— One-year goals
— Three-year goals

One-month goals: These allow you to plan specific actions you can take daily to reach a short-term goal. These are meant to be practical and attainable.

One-year goals: Consider the consequences of your one- month goals: where could you be if these are accomplished? What are the next steps? What must you do? How many people must you mobilize to be part of your team to ensure that your dream progresses?

Three-year goals: This is the place for vision building. As you meditate on God's purposes for your dream, prayerfully consider where He could take you. As you write your three-year goals, they may seem outrageous or impossible. Remember that you serve the Creator of the universe and claim Philippians 4:13, "I can do everything through Him who gives me strength."

During the development of my dream of reaching women around the world through the Internet, my goals were consistently met and exceeded by God's grace.

One of the initial goals I set for our team was to see 1,000 hits per day on the evangelistic Website. It took some time and a lot of hard work for us to meet that goal. Once we were focused on consistently doing our part, though, God blessed us by radically exceeding our expectations. As this book is written, *Women Today Magazine* receives over 50,000 hits per day.

I had a longer-term goal to get other Christians excited about the Internet and the possibilities for evangelism in cyberspace. Consequently, I took every opportunity to share what God had laid on my heart and to share the amazing things He had done through our ministry and others like it.

One woman I know, a long-time friend of Crusade ministries, was initially very concerned about having the Internet in her home. As a parent, she wasn't certain that this technology could have any value to a Christian family—or to a Christian woman. Timidly at first, she began to explore chat rooms. Almost immediately, God brought her into contact with women whose needs she could have a part in meeting. She discovered that she could have a private discussion with one of the other visitors to the chat room, pray for or with someone, challenge a doubter or direct someone to a website where she might get some answers. With great anticipation, she now prayerfully engages in evangelism online, rejoicing in every life the Lord is touching through her.

Three-year goals are perhaps the most exciting for me. As I looked toward the future, I had a vision of women everywhere having access to the gospel on the Internet and sharing with each other. If every woman who visited the *Women Today Magazine* and *Christian Women Today* Websites shared what she had found with two friends, the multiplication would be staggering.

Take Mericiel, for instance, who wrote to the Women Today Online staff from her home in the Philippines.

"I found your site very helpful to everyone, specially your topic about 'Beginning your Journey of Joy'," she wrote. "I'm an ordinary Christian and only two years in my faith. I really love to serve the Lord and share His Word of salvation to others but I still don't have the skills to do it. Your material is an answered prayer to me."

I was delighted to hear that the Websites had helped Mericiel. I was even more delighted by her unusual request.

"I would like to ask your permission if I can use this topic, print it and post it in our bulletin board here in our restaurant," she continued. "I would like to print it and use it in sharing the gospel if ever you will allow me. I know we have the same heart and goal, to share the gospel to everybody, to serve and to please our Lord."

Indeed we do! Who could say no to such a sweet desire to serve the Lord? Mericiel's excitement about sharing what she had learned is the best possible fulfillment of the passion God had laid on my heart. In working towards our shorter-term goals—providing spiritual food for Mericiel—we met a long-term goal by providing her with the tools she needed to take the truth to those in her own sphere of influence. We continue to receive many similar requests.

[1] From an interview with Silken Lauman in the Summer, 1997 issue of Action Bulletin, a publication of the Association for the Advancement of Women and Sport and Physical Activity, www.caaws.ca/Action/summer97/silken.htm

ACTION POINTS

1. What are your one-month goals? What steps will you take in this time? Be sure to note your commitments in your appointment book.

_____
_____
_____
_____
_____
_____
_____
_____
_____
_____
_____

2. What do you want to accomplish in the next year?

_____
_____
_____
_____
_____
_____
_____
_____
_____
_____
_____
_____

3. What is your vision for the future of your dream? Write down your three-year goals and be sure to keep this list handy.

_____

_____

_____

_____

_____

_____

_____

_____

_____

_____

_____

_____

_____

_____

_____

_____

_____

_____

_____

_____

_____

_____

_____

_____

_____

_____

_____

_____

_____

_____

_____

_____

"All your dreams can come true ...

if you have the courage to pursue them."

WALT DISNEY

CHAPTER SEVEN

Stay Organized and On Track

S YOUR GOALS ARE MET AND YOU SET NEW ONES, IT would be easy to lose sight of the structure of your dream. To be certain that you are running the same race you started, it is vital to be organized and keep good records.

Because I wanted to be more involved in ministering to women, I knew my life had to be more organized. I set my sights on becoming that ideal woman in Proverbs 31. I didn't feel comfortable doing ministry unless my own home was in order. While pursuing God-sized dreams, I wanted to make sure I also stayed on top of housework. I found a book called *Side-tracked Home Executives* written by Pam Young and Peggy Jones. This book helped me create and implement an organized system to ensure my house was cleaned thoroughly. Some jobs were done daily, some weekly, some monthly and some annually.

I have followed this system for many years. Although I changed some of it as I entered the different seasons of my life—the principles remained the same.

When our children were teens and at home, we cleaned house on Saturday morning. Each of us had to clean a designated room. I also hired a cleaning woman to help whenever I could not keep up.

As the children finished school and left home, I hired a cleaning woman to come in for several hours each week, but I always did the deep cleaning tasks myself. I still do.

It was this organized system and plan to keep my house in order that enabled me to pursue other dreams. Having a plan and measurable goals with time limits will help you make your dream come true.

You need to know where you have been and where you are going to keep your dream on track. The notes you have made working through this book can help you get started.

Know Where You Have Been

It is important to record the steps you have taken to reach your goals. Doing what God has called you to do places you at risk. Satan will attack where he can. If you can turn a page and point to the prayer, meditation and Scripture that formed the foundation of your dream, you will not easily be swayed from your path.

Keep your notes where they will be preserved but are easy to access. This may be in your computer, on paper in a filing cabinet, a computer disc or CD-ROM. Keep a detailed daily scheduler. If you are like me, you may have a combination of all the above. Regardless of the method, keep track of your dream, the measurable goals and the progress. Allow yourself the luxury of revisiting the birth of your dream from time to time. Rejoice in the seed God planted and how He has caused it to grow.

Every year between Christmas and New Year Day, I revisit my goals. I praise God for what He has done and adjust the measurable goals for the coming year.

Increase Your Vision

Keeping records allows you to see what goals have been met as the Lord develops your dream. It also allows you to increase your vision as you set new goals.

As I look back at the things I thought might happen as a result of our ministry on the Internet, I realized that in some ways I had not been expecting enough. Not that any of us should be so presumptuous as to demand things from the Lord, but we are told to expect an amazing outcome when He is working through us.

> *"Believe me when I say that I am in the Father and the Father is in me; or at least believe on the evidence of the miracles themselves. I tell you the truth, anyone who has faith in me will do what I have been doing. He will do even greater things than these, because I am going to the Father. And I will do whatever you ask in my name, so that the Son may bring glory to the Father. You may ask me for anything in my name, and I will do it."*
>
> JOHN 14:11-14

As I looked at how the Internet ministry had grown, I could see that God was answering prayers much bigger than those we had been praying. This allowed us to increase our goals, in faith, and trust Him for the results of the work He'd given us to do.

Know Where You Are Going

Staying organized and keeping records allows you to be certain of the decisions you make for the future. To begin the process of accomplishing your dream, you needed to clarify your passion and focus on God's desire for your life. As you look back over the goals you have set and the records of how they have been met, it will be easier to determine which decisions are most likely to lead to the fulfillment of this Christ-centered dream and which are not.

On a personal level, this kind of organization means that I keep a detailed daily planner. All of my appointments, short and long-term goals and responsibilities are recorded here. This allows me not only to be certain that I do not miss meetings or lose dates, but also to see how the Lord answers my prayers and continues to challenge me to grow.

As a ministry working on the Internet we are fortunate to have excellent programs to record our progress. We can see how many visitors we receive, how long they stay, what they read and when they leave. We can even tell what countries they come from. Similarly, we have records of our early work—what it looked like, what changes we made and why. We can even read old email messages. These records are invaluable as we work together as a team to plan for future growth.

There are almost as many possibilities for growth in our ministry as there are days in the year. One very clear path that has evolved seems to be the translation of Women Today Internet resources into other languages. Diverse cultural and linguistic communities are flourishing on the Web. Although the Women Today Websites have made significant inroads into countries where the first language is not English, Michelle's story (see Chapter four) is a wonderful encouragement to serve women in their own languages.

The Spanish-speaking world also has a very high profile on the Internet. With this in mind we have moved forward with the translation of the gospel presentation and many of the articles and testimonies into Spanish. Even as this book is being published, we are exploring partnerships in Latin America for using the translated content. Similarly, the number of Chinese Internet users, Websites and search engines is increasing. I have a passion to see the development of Women Today's Internet resources in many languages in partnership with others. A realization of this dream came when a Webmaster from a women's Website in Hong Kong asked to use our material. I have found that God doesn't necessarily expect me to be responsible for all these languages. He has His qualified people in place all over the world.

The interest we have seen among Internet users in Arabic countries has been most interesting. Two women's Websites in the Middle East are positioning our evangelistic website right on their home page. Many of the people who have computers in the Middle East speak and read English. It is very rewarding to see how God is engineering the promotion of our Websites.

Planning for the future is a constant thrilling challenge. What is God doing? What does He want us to do next? Where and how can we be most effective? We bring the Websites before the Lord each day—asking for wisdom, direction and fruit.

As we keep statistics, read the exciting letters from our users and evaluate our progress, we are better able to determine what is most important and which steps to take next.

ACTION POINTS

1. Record your goals and keep them for future reference. As you make plans for the future, review the things you wanted to achieve and by what date. Look back to see how God met or exceeded these goals. Are your goals God-sized goals, based on what you know He would like you to visualize? Or are you setting goals that are "practical" and "realistic" based on what you think you can do?

_____

_____

_____

_____

2. Find and utilize a system of organization that works for you. Try and be faithful to maintain it. If you like to keep records on paper in a filing cabinet, do it. If a computer works better for you, great—but be sure to back up your files!

3. Keep an orderly personal schedule, whether in a daily planner, on sticky notes around your computer screen or on a palm pilot. Record all appointments and important dates (such as the dates of goals you have set). You may also wish to keep contact information for colleagues and associates here.

4. Track the progress of your goals.
   — Where did you intend to be by now?

_____

_____

_____

— What goals have been met?

_____

_____

_____

— What goals require more planning, time or revision?

_____

_____

_____

— How has God been faithful to meet your needs?

_____

_____

_____

5. Clarify your direction for the future.
   — What new goals must be set?

_____

_____

_____

— How does God want to increase your vision, as you set new goals and trust Him to meet your needs?

_____

_____

_____

_____

"No horse gets anywhere until he is harnessed.

No steam or gas engine drives anything until it is

confined. No Niagara is ever turned into light and

power until it is tunneled. No life ever grows great until

it is focused, dedicated, disciplined."

HARRY EMERSON FODSICK

Conclusion

RE YOU EXCITED?

I hope you are. The thoughts, ideas and passions that have been stirring at the back of your mind can be so much more. God is faithful to complete what He begins in each of us, and there is nothing more exciting than seeing another clear step on that path. I believe that you will come away from this book with exactly what He knows you need. Press on; don't let the fire grow cold.

Do you feel motivated to seek God's will for your life?

I hope you do. It is my prayer that the simple steps outlined in this book will provide you with a framework for accomplishing your dream. Even more importantly, I pray that you will take the opportunity to surrender yourself to Christ as the Lord of your life. Whether or not you have a dream to accomplish right now, you can always have a deeply intimate relationship with the Lord and a life daily directed by the Holy Spirit. Press on; seek to know Him more.

Will you take the first step?

I hope you will. The first step can be the most frightening. Yet the rewards far outweigh the cost.

If you have seen the movie "Indiana Jones and the Last Crusade,"¹ you will recall the "tests" the intrepid archeologist faced as he sought the Holy Grail. The final test was one of faith. He stared out across a chasm he could never jump across. There was no bridge, no visible means to get the other side. He had to have faith, as he stepped blindly out into the abyss, that there would be something beneath his feet. And there was.

Indiana Jones is a fictional character who stumbles upon a lesson in faith while seeking something else. Yet the lesson is one we should be familiar with. The Bible is full of similar examples:

- Mary, the mother of Jesus, trusted God 's word that said she would conceive when the Holy Spirit came upon her.
- Abraham took Isaac to be sacrificed to the Lord.
- Moses returned to Egypt to ask Pharaoh to release the Israelites.
- Peter stepped out of the boat into a raging sea to join Christ walking upon the waves.
- Stephen surrendered himself to death by stoning, certain of the bliss that awaited him.
- Paul acted in obedience to the Lord and presented himself as a minister of the gospel to the very people he had persecuted?

When we are certain of the foundation upon which our faith is built—Christ Himself—we can step out into the abyss in faith and be equally certain that there will be something beneath our feet. Press out in faith. Trust your dream to the Lord and He will see it to completion.

God bless you!

I would love to hear how God has used your dream for His purposes. Please write to me at:
katherine@mkehler.com

---

[1] "Indiana Jones and the Last Crusade," released by Paramount Pictures, Lucasfilm Ltd., 1989.

"Not that I have already obtained all this,

or have already been made perfect, but I press on

to take hold of that for which Christ Jesus

took hold of me. Brothers, I do not consider myself

yet to have taken hold of it. But one thing I do:

Forgetting what is behind and straining toward

what is ahead, I press on toward the goal to win

the prize for which God has called me heavenward

in Christ Jesus."

[PHILIPPIANS 3:12-14]

Have You Made the Wonderful Discovery of the Spirit-filled Life?

Every day can be an exciting adventure for the Christian who knows the reality of being filled with the Holy Spirit and who lives constantly, moment by moment, under His gracious direction.

The Bible Tells Us That There Are Three Kinds of People

Natural Man (One who has not received Christ)
"A natural man does not accept the things of the Spirit of God; for they are foolishness to him, and he cannot understand them, because they are spiritually appraised" (1 CORINTHIANS 2:14).

Spiritual Man (One who is directed and empowered by the Holy Spirit)
"He who is spiritual appraises all things... We have the mind of Christ" (1 CORINTHIANS 2:15).

Carnal Man (One who has received Christ, but who lives in defeat because is trying to live the Christian life in his own strength)
"And I brethren, could not speak to you as to spiritual men, but as to carnal men, as to babes in Christ. I gave you milk to drink, not solid food; for you were not yet able to receive it. Indeed, even now you are not yet able, for you are still carnal. For since there is jealousy and strife among you, are you not fleshy, and are you not walking like mere men?" (1 CORINTHIANS 3:1-3).

God Has Provided For Us an Abundant and Fruitful Christian Life

Jesus said, "I came that they might have life, and might have it abundantly" (JOHN 10:10).

"I am the vine, you are the branches; he who abides in Me, and I in him, he bears much fruit; for apart from Me you can do nothing" (JOHN 15:5).

"But the fruit of the spirit is love, joy, peace, patience, kindness, goodness, faithfulness, gentleness, self-control; against such things there is no law" (GALATIANS 5:22, 23).

"But you shall receive power when the Holy Spirit has come upon you; and shall be My witnesses both in Jerusalem, and in all Judea and Samaria, and even to the remotest part of the earth" (ACTS 1:8).

The Spiritual Man — Some spiritual traits which result from trusting God:

- Love
- Peace
- Kindness ·
- Goodness
- Empowered by Holy Spirit
- Has effective prayer life
- Trusts God

- Joy
- Patience
- Faithfulness
- Life is Christ-centered
- Introduces others to Christ
- Understands God's Word
- Obeys God

The degree to which these traits are manifested in your life depends upon the extent to which you trust the Lord with every detail of your life, and upon your maturity in Christ. If you are only beginning to understand the ministry of the Holy Spirit, don't be discouraged if you are not as fruitful as more mature Christians who have known and experienced this truth for a longer period.

Why is it that most Christians are not experiencing the abundant life?

Carnal Christians Cannot Experience the Abundant and Fruitful Christian Life
· The carnal person trusts in her own efforts to live the Christian life: she is either uninformed about, or has forgotten, God's love, forgiveness, and power (ROMANS 5:8-10; HEBREWS 10:1-25; 1 JOHN 1; 2:1-3; 2 PETER 1:9; ACTS 1:8).
· She has an up-and-down spiritual experience.
· She cannot understand herself - she wants to do what is right, but cannot.
· She fails to draw upon the power of the Holy Spirit to live the Christian life.
(1 CORINTHIANS 3:1-3; ROMANS 7:15-24; 8:7; GALATIANS 5:16-18)

The Carnal Man — Some or all of the following traits may characterize the Christian who does not fully trust God:

- · Legalistic attitude
- · Jealousy
- · Worry
- · Discouragement
- · Aimlessness
- · Ignorance of spiritual heritage
- · Disobedience
- · Guilt
- · Impure thoughts
- · Frustration
- · Critical spirit
- · Fear
- · Unbelief
- · Poor prayer life
- · Loss of love for Christ and for others
- · No desire for bible study

(The individual who professes to be a Christian but who continues to practice sin should realize that she may not be a Christian at all, according to 1 JOHN 2:3; 3:6, 9; EPHESIANS 5:5).

The third truth gives us the only solution to this problem...

Jesus Promised the Abundant and Fruitful Life as the Result of Being Filled (Directed and Empowered) by the Holy Spirit
     The Spirit-filled life is the Christ-directed life by which Christ lives His life in and through us in the power of the Holy Spirit (JOHN 15).
     A person becomes a Christian through the ministry of the

Holy Spirit, according to John 3:1-8. From the moment of spiritual birth, the Christian is indwelt by the Holy Spirit at all times (JOHN 1:12; COLOSSIANS 2:9, 10; JOHN 14:16, 17). Though all Christians are indwelt by the Holy Spirit, not all Christians are filled (directed and empowered) by the Holy Spirit.

The Holy Spirit is the source of the overflowing life (JOHN 7:37-39).

The Holy Spirit came to glorify Christ (JOHN 16:1-15). When a person is filled with the Holy Spirit, she is a true disciple of Christ.

In His last command before His ascension, Christ promised the power of the Holy Spirit to enable us to be witnesses for Him (ACTS 1:1-9).

How, then, can one be filled with the Holy Spirit?

We are filled by the Holy Spirit by faith; then we can experience the abundant and fruitful life which Christ promised to each Christian.

You can appropriate the filling of the Holy Spirit right now if you:

Sincerely desire to be directed and empowered by the Holy Spirit (MATTHEW 5:6; JOHN 7:37-39).

Confess your sins. By faith thank God that He has forgiven all of your sins—past, present and future—because Christ died for you (COLOSSIANS 2:13-15; I JOHN I; 2:1-3; HEBREWS 10:1-17).

Present every area of your life to God (ROMANS 12:1, 2).

By faith claim the fullness of the Holy Spirit, according to:

His Command - Be filled with the Spirit. *"And do not get drunk with wine, for that is dissipation, but be filled with the Spirit"* (EPHESIANS 5:18).

His Promise - He will always answer when we pray according to His will. *"And this is the confidence which we have before Him, that, if we ask anything according to His will, He hears us. And if we know that He hears us in whatever we ask, we know that we have the requests which we have asked of Him."* (I JOHN 5:14, 15).

Faith can be expressed through prayer...

How to Pray in Faith to be Filled with the Holy Spirit
We are filled with the Holy Spirit by faith alone. However, true prayer is one way of expressing your faith. The following is a suggested prayer:

"Dear Father, I need You. I acknowledge that I have been directing my own life and that, as a result, I have sinned against You. I thank You that You have forgiven my sins through Christ's death on the cross for me. I now invite Christ to again take His place on the throne of my life. Fill me with the Holy Spirit as You commanded me to be filled, and as You promised in Your Word that You would do if I asked in faith. I now thank You for directing my life and for filling me with the Holy Spirit."

Does this prayer express the desire of your heart? If so, bow in prayer and trust God to fill you with the Holy Spirit right now.

If you prayed this prayer, let us know. We will be happy to answer your questions and send you more information about growing in your relationship with Jesus Christ.

How to Know That You are Filled (Directed and Empowered) with the Holy Spirit
Did you ask God to fill you with the Holy Spirit? Do you know that you are now filled with the Holy Spirit? On what authority? (On the trustworthiness of God Himself and His Word: HEBREWS 11:6; ROMANS 14:22, 23.)

Do not depend upon feelings. The promise of God's Word, not our feelings, is our authority. The Christian lives by faith (trust) in the trustworthiness of God Himself and His Word. This train diagram illustrates the relationship between fact (God and His Word), faith (our trust in God and His Word), and feeling (the result of our faith and obedience) (JOHN 14:21).

The train will run with or without the caboose. However, it would be futile to attempt to pull the train by the caboose. In the same way, we, as Christians, do not depend upon feelings or emotions, but we place our faith (trust) in the trustworthiness of God and the promises of His Word.

How to Walk in the Spirit

Faith (trust in God and in His promises) is the only means by which a Christian can live the Spirit-directed life. As you continue to trust Christ moment by moment:

Your life will demonstrate more and more of the fruit of the Spirit (GALATIANS 5:22, 23) and will be more and more conformed to the image of Christ (ROMANS 12:2; 2 CORINTHIANS 3:18).

Your prayer life and study of God's Word will become more meaningful.

You will experience His power in witnessing (ACTS 1:8).

You will be prepared for spiritual conflict against the world (1 JOHN 2:15-17); against the flesh (GALATIANS 5:16-17); and against Satan (1 PETER 5:7-9; EPHESIANS 6:10- 13).

You will experience His power to resist temptation and sin (1 CORINTHIANS 10:13; PHILIPPIANS 4:13; EPHESIANS 1:19-23; 2 TIMOTHY 1:7; ROMANS 6:1-16).

Spiritual Breathing

By faith you can continue to experience God's love and forgiveness.

If you become aware of an area of your life (an attitude or an action) that is displeasing to the Lord, even though you are walking with Him and sincerely desiring to serve Him, simply thank God that He has forgiven your sins —past, present and future— on the basis of Christ's death on the cross. Claim His love and forgiveness by faith and continue to have fellowship with Him.

If you retake the throne of your life through sin— a definite act of disobedience—breathe spiritually.

Spiritual breathing (exhaling the impure and inhaling the pure) is an exercise in faith that enables you to continue to experience God's love and forgiveness.

Exhale—confess your sin—agree with God concerning your sin and thank Him for His forgiveness of it, according to I JOHN 1:9 and HEBREWS 10:1-25. Confession involves repentance—a change in attitude and action.

Inhale—surrender the control of your life to Christ, and appropriate (receive) the fullness of the Holy Spirit by faith. Trust that He now directs and empowers you; according to the command of EPHESIANS 5:18, and the promise of I JOHN 5:14, 15.

You will want to share this important discovery...
If this has been meaningful and helpful to you, please share it with someone else. If you have questions or comments, please email us at editor@womentodaymagazine.com
or katherine@mkehler.com

Written by Dr. Bill Bright © 1995-1997 Campus Crusade for Christ International Questions and Comments are always welcome!

The Websites God Grew

You, too, can point people to Christ using Webcards

Women Today Magazine was recently ranked as one of the top ten Websites for women—just three spots behind the online version of *Good Housekeeping*. Using the topics of the day as a starting point, it offers readers informative and engaging content from a Christian perspective. The articles in the life stories section detail one woman's encounter with Christ and each one includes a gospel presentation and an opportunity to pray. All articles are connected to gospel presentations through links, related stories and side bar content. Non-threatening and highly approachable, *Women Today Magazine* is an easy way to expose a friend to a Christian viewpoint. See www.womentodaymagazine.com.

Women Today Magazine is also available in French. See www.femmesaujourdhui.com.

Journey of Joy contains an online presentation of the gospel according to Campus Crusade for Christ's *Four Spiritual Laws*, repackaged specifically for women. Using the popular topic of self-esteem as a starting point, *Journey of Joy* takes visitors through the *Four Laws* to show that true meaning and value come from a personal relationship with Jesus Christ. Interactive, non-threatening and easy to follow, *Journey of Joy* also includes follow-up materials such as inductive Bible studies, the *Knowing Jesus Personally* magazine, a form to ask questions and an email mentoring program. See www.journeyofjoy.com.

Christian Women Today focuses on discipling and

training. Holy Spirit testimonies challenge and encourage readers while articles on prayer and practical evangelism provide the necessary tools to take the gospel around the block and around the world. *Christian Women Today's* magazine format makes everything easy to find, and with free recipes and jokes you can share anywhere, there really is something for everyone. Be sure to visit the chatroom which features a weekly schedule of directed, moderated chats and our short daily devotions. See www.christianwomentoday.com.

Want to "increase your territory" and expose your neighbors to Christ? Webcards are a very easy and effective method to use. Printed on business card-sized paper, you can carry these anywhere, Webcards contain the site's address and a brief description. Pass them out to co-workers, leave some at the café, doctor's office or at the gym. Tack a few on the community bulletin board—the possibilities are endless.

A Webcard is like a business card advertising a Website.

Webcards are available for all four sites: *Women Today Magazine*, *Christian Women Today*, *Femmes Aujourd'hui* and *Journey of Joy*.

You can order 100 Webcards for only $5.00 (Cdn), excludes shipping.

> Mail: New Life Resouces
>   Box 300, Vancouver, BC
>   V6C 2X3
> Email: orders@crusade.org
> Phone: 1-800-667-0558
> Fax: 1-800-665-8480

About the Authors

KATHERINE JANE KEHLER
25557 Fraser Highway
Langley, BC V4W 1Z9
katherine@mkehler.com

Born in Bassano, Alberta, Katherine's family moved to the Fraser Valley in British Columbia when she was in the third grade and she has made this area her home ever since.

She has been married to Marvin for over 45 years—they have four grown children and their ninth grandchild was born in July 1999.

She has always been interested in helping women around the world reach their maximum potential and has initiated and organized many seminars, conferences and workshops toward this end. She has also written many short inspirational articles evolving from her life's experience and faith in God.

Having a global vision, she has traveled extensively internationally and has been the keynote speaker at events for government, business and professional women in Nigeria, Zimbabwe, Russia, Ukraine, Germany, Costa Rica, Mexico, the United States and Canada.

In 1976 she began Canadian Prayer Alert, a Campus Crusade ministry that mobilized people across Canada to pray for government leaders.

In the early 90's, she initiated a strategy, Women in Leadership, to help influential women examine the spiritual side of their lives. A few years later, Women Today Canada began.

She is the executive editor of *Women Today* magazine which is distributed in over 140 countries.

In 1995 she began a Website version of the magazine, entitled *Women Today Magazine*. As time went on, together with a team of talented staff, they expanded to five Websites, in both English and French. Now, over 100,000 women from over 155 countries visit their sites every month.

She works hard and trusts God for the impossible.

For relaxation, she enjoys reading, gardening and handwork.

RUTHANN RAYCROFT

RuthAnn Raycroft was born on January 10, 1970 in Saskatoon, Saskatchewan in Canada. The youngest of three children, RuthAnn relocated to Edmonton with her family in 1971. She lived in Edmonton until 1995, obtaining her high school diploma from Strathcona Christian Academy in 1987, visual arts training at Grant MacEwan Community College in 1990 and a Bachelor of Arts degree (with distinction) in English and Political Science from Concordia University College of Alberta in 1994. Longing to study abroad, RuthAnn was accepted at several universities in the UK and the Republic of Ireland for graduate studies. She received her Master of Arts degree in English Literature from Cardiff University (University of Wales, College of Cardiff) in 1996. Returning to Canada to live in British Columbia's Lower Mainland, RuthAnn was the senior writer and editor for two women's Websites from 1998-2000. Her work on *Women Today Magazine* and *Christian Women Today* has been read in over 155 countries around the world. RuthAnn loves the outdoors, art, theatre, making anything with her own two hands and the written word. She loves music and delights in singing whenever she has the opportunity.

rraycroft@canada.com

Women Today Online is a Great Investment Now and For All Eternity

Just over a year ago, on the advice of a financial advisor, I invested a sum of money toward my retirement. Within one year this sum grew by 30 percent. Needless to say, I was very pleased with the return on my investment.

In light of eternity, giving to the ministry of Women Today Online, a ministry of Campus Crusade for Christ, Canada, is a great investment. Not only for changed lives here on earth, but for the women from 155 different countries who will spend eternity in heaven because they are introduced to Jesus Christ through our Websites.

In four consecutive years the number of women reached with the gospel and built in their faith through the Websites have doubled. In the last 12 months over 200,000 gospel presentations and more than 300,000 articles were read. Women seeking counsel read over 9,000 biblically-based responses by Dr. Ginger Gabriel in just one month.

The cost of exposures to the gospel worked out to 40 cents per exposure. The cost for discipling women was less then 37 cents for each article read.

When we began this Internet ministry six years ago, God touched a handful of men and women who recognized the potential of the Internet to help accelerate the fulfillment of our Lord's Great Commission. "Therefore go and make disciples of all nations, baptizing them in the name of the Father and of the Son and of the Holy Spirit, and teaching them to obey everything I have commanded you." Matthew 28:19 - 20. They invested their L (labor), I (influence) F (finance) and E (expertise) and God multiplied their investment far beyond our dreams or prayers.

Because of the tremendous growth of our Websites, we are asking God to raise up more people so that together we can capture the opportunities God provides through the Internet ministry.

Are you willing to become involved with us? Will you pray and ask God if He would have you invest your L.I.F.E. to help reach the world through the Internet? Perhaps you want to be involved personally or perhaps you want to use your influence and finances. There are many ways in which you can be involved:

— **Labor** - are you willing to commit one or more hours per week to hostess a chat room session?

— **Influence** - would you use your influence to mobilize other women to become involved?

— **Finance** - would you funnel some of your finances to allow more women to experience the touch of Jesus?

— **Expertise** - are you a web designer, programmer, marketer, writer or an editor? Or do you have any talents you are willing to volunteer for the expansion of God's kingdom?

If God prompts you to help in one or more of these areas, please contact me.

Thank you and may God bless you!

Katherine Kehler
Director, Women Today Online

Call me at: 604-514-2000 ext. 196
Email: katherine@mkehler.com
Address: Women Today Online,
Campus Crusade for Christ, Canada
Box 300, Vancouver, BC V6C 2X3

Women Today

A Magazine with a Purpose

It all boils down to what's important to you.

Women Today addresses issues that matter to women. But more to the point, it is written and put together for the express purpose of letting you share Jesus with women who don't know Him. It's the perfect gift to give someone who has everything except God— or someone who has nothing and needs God. If you've got a colleague or a neighbor who fits that description, order as many copies of *Women Today* as you have friends. *Women Today* isn't just a magazine, it's a giveaway about who Jesus is. If it's important for you to share Him with your friends, it's important for you to call for your copies today.

Order today!

By Phone: 1-800-667-0558
By Fax: 1-800-665-8480
By E-mail: orders@crusade.org

Quantity	Price per copy
1	$2.95
2-49	$2.50
50+	$2.25

Prices do not include shipping and GST.

Women Today Canada

Box 300, Vancouver, BC V6C 2X3

Email: wtsource@crusade.org

ISBN 155212731-1

9 781552 127315